TECH BYTES
EXPLORING SPACE

LIFE ON MARS

BY JOYCE MARKOVICS

Norwood House Press

NORWOOD HOUSE PRESS

Cover: An artist's concept showing the InSight lander, its sensors, cameras, and instruments.

For more information about Norwood House Press, please visit our website at: www.norwoodhousepress.com or call 866-565-2900.

Book Designer: Ed Morgan
Editorial and Production: Bowerbird Books
Content Consultant: Dr. Joel Green, Astrophysicist

Photo Credits: NASA/JPL-Caltech, cover and title page; NASA, 4; NASA, 5; NASA, 6; © Sundry Photography/Shutterstock, 7; NASA/JPL-Caltech/ASU/MSSS, 8; NASA/JPL-Caltech, 9; ESA & MPS for OSIRIS Team MPS/UPD/LAM/IAA/RSSD/INTA/UPM/DASP/IDA, 10 (Mars); freepik.com, 10–11 (Earth); freepik.com, 11 bottom; NASA/JPL-Caltech, 12; NASA/JPL-Caltech/University of Arizona, 13; Public Domain, 14; Public Domain, 15; NASA, 16; Public Domain, 17; NASA, 18; NASA/JPL, 19; NASA, 20; NASA, 21; NASA, 22–23; NASA, 23 inset; NASA/GSFC, 16; NASA/JPL, 25; NASA, 26; NASA, 27; NASA, 28; NASA/JPL/Malin Space Science Systems, 29; NASA/JPL/Cornell University, Maas Digital LLC, 30; NASA/JPL-Caltech/Cornell/ASU, 31; NASA, 32; NASA, 33; NASA/JPL-Caltech, 34; NASA, 35; NASA, 36–27; Unsplash.com, 38; NASA/JPL-Caltech, 39; Wikimedia Commons/ Jared Krahn, 40; NASA, 41; freepik.com, 42–43.

Copyright © 2023 Norwood House Press

Hardcover ISBN: 978-1-68450-730-6
Paperback ISBN: 978-1-68404-836-6

All rights reserved. No part of this book may be reproduced or utilized in any form or by any means without written permission from the publisher.

Library of Congress Cataloging-in-Publication Data has been filed and is available at catalog.loc.gov

359N—012023
Manufactured in the United States of America in North Mankato, Minnesota.

CONTENTS

CHAPTER 1
Looking for Life 4

CHAPTER 2
Investigating Mars 10

CHAPTER 3
Life on Mars? 22

CHAPTER 4
Future Exploration 36

Glossary   44
For More Information   46
Index   48
About the Author   48

Words that are bolded in the text are defined in the glossary.

CHAPTER 1
LOOKING for LIFE

After an almost 300-million-mile (483-million-km) trip from Earth, the newest **NASA** robotic vehicle, or rover, neared Mars's **atmosphere**. It was February 18, 2021. The car-sized rover named Perseverance, or Percy for short, had traveled through space enclosed in a protective case called an aeroshell. Percy's onboard technology would help the rover steer itself and avoid danger. As it zipped through the extremely hot Martian atmosphere at 12,000 miles per hour (19,312 kph), a heat shield prevented the rover from burning up.

This image shows Perseverance about to touch down on Mars. The rover cost about $2.7 billion to build. It's packed with tools and technology to explore Mars.

When Percy was about 7 miles (11 km) above the ground, it used **radar** to detect how far it was from the surface of Mars, also known as the Red Planet. Then the rover **deployed** a parachute to help it slow down and stop it from smashing into the surface of Mars. Rockets known as jetpacks fired in reverse to further decrease Percy's speed. The landing would take about seven minutes, which the guidance team at the Jet Propulsion Laboratory back on Earth called "seven minutes of terror." Many things could go wrong—and all the team could do was hope for the best.

An illustration of the Perseverance rover landing on Mars

DID YOU KNOW?

Because of Mars's distance from Earth, radio signals take more than 11 minutes to reach Mars. In other words, when Percy began sending messages back about the landing, the spacecraft had already been on Mars for four minutes!

Thanks to Percy's computers and other technology, the guidance team at Jet Propulsion Laboratory on Earth, and a lot of good luck, the landing went smoothly! The most advanced space **probe** ever built safely touched down on Mars at 3:44 PM on February 18. The team back on Earth clapped and cheered. "Perseverance will get you anywhere," they joked after the successful landing. "Now the fun really starts," said another NASA scientist anticipating all the discoveries the rover would make.

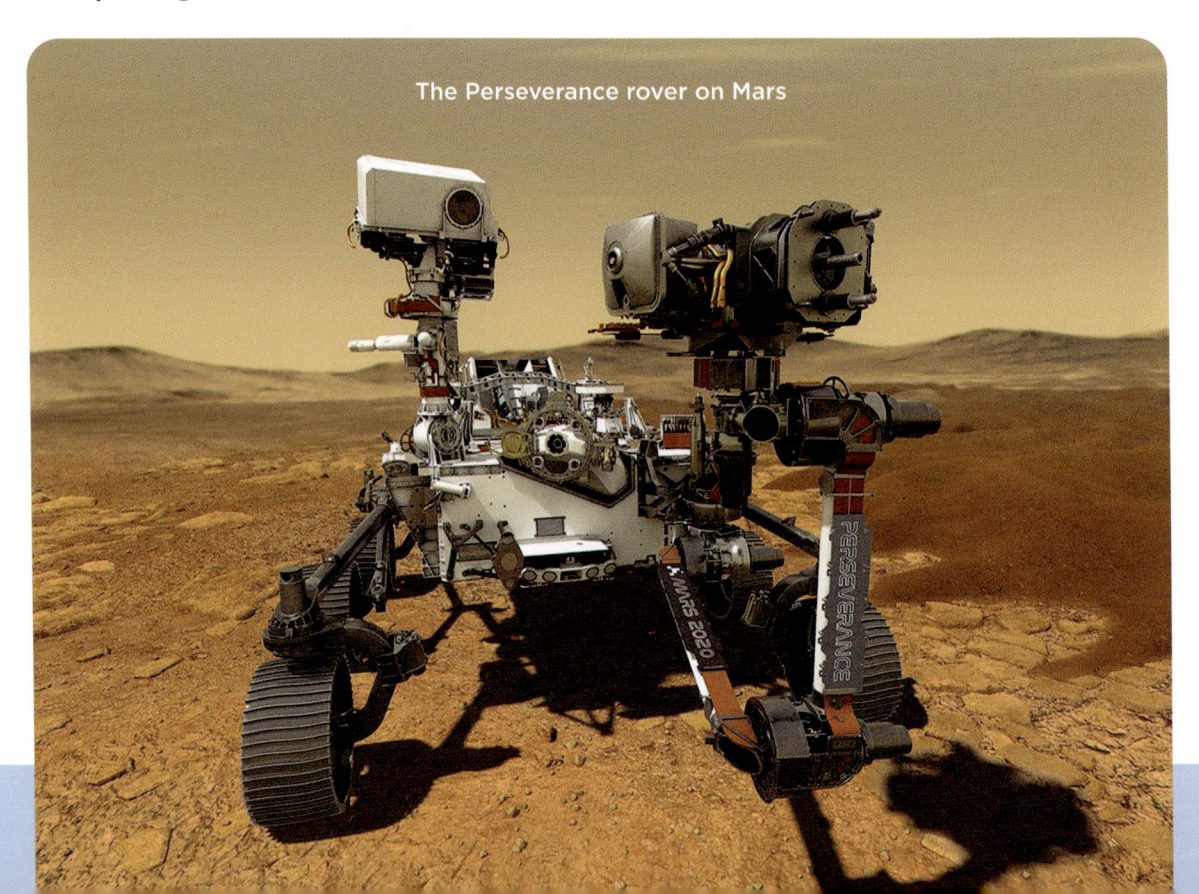

The Perseverance rover on Mars

The Perseverance rover is on an amazing years-long mission. The main goal is to answer key questions about Mars: Was there ever life on the planet, and could humans live on Mars in the future? Percy is specially designed to hunt for signs of ancient living things. The rover carries state-of-the-art technology, including cameras to photograph the planet, radar that can pierce through solid ground, and lasers that can identify the chemical makeup of Martian rocks. Percy will also conduct a variety of experiments to find out, for example, how to make oxygen from the harsh Martian atmosphere to possibly support life one day. It will also collect rock samples that might contain signs of life, which will eventually be analyzed back on Earth.

A control room in the Jet Propulsion Laboratory

DID YOU KNOW?

The Jet Propulsion Laboratory (JPL) is located in Pasadena, California. It's a NASA/Caltech research center that carries out robotic space missions. JPL created the first satellite that orbits Earth. It also developed NASA's Deep Space Network. This network of antennas spread around the world communicates with interplanetary spacecraft.

The Perseverance rover landed in the Jezero Crater, the toughest Martian **terrain** any NASA rover has ever landed on. It started snapping pictures immediately. The crater is a large 28-mile- (45-km-) wide area in the northern part of Mars. It's filled with rocks, boulders, sand, and swirling clouds of rust-colored dust. The Jezero Crater wasn't always a giant dusty hollow, however. About three billion years ago, scientists believe it was a deep lake near a flowing river. They know this from previous spacecraft missions that took images of the area, which look exactly like dry lakes and riverbeds on Earth. The boulders strewn across the dry Martian lakebed were likely carried by water. There are also layers of **sediment** similar to that found in lakes on Earth. For life to exist anywhere, water is needed. Scientists wonder whether the lake and surrounding area might have supported life. It's a perfect place to look for fossilized **microbes**. "I think that has to be the hands-down most exciting thing," said planetary scientist Tim Goudge.

An image of the Jezero Crater taken by Percy

NAME THAT NASA ROVER!

The Perseverance rover

There have been five NASA rovers, all with different names. The Curiosity rover landed on the Red Planet in 2012. Before that came Spirit and Opportunity, which both landed in 2004, and Sojourner, which landed in 1997. So how does NASA choose a name for a rover? NASA asks children for help! In March 2020, seventh-grader Alex Mather learned that the name Perseverance he chose for the next rover had been selected from 28,000 entries. Alex was thrilled. When asked how he felt about winning, Alex said, "This Mars rover will help pave the way for human presence there and I wanted to try and help in any way I could."

CHAPTER 2
INVESTIGATING
MARS

Mars is the fourth planet from the Sun and the easiest to spot in the sky because of its red color. After Mercury, it's the second-smallest planet in our solar system. If you sliced Mars in half, it would measure 4,224 miles (6,798 km) from one side to the other. That makes it about half the size of Earth. Like Earth, Mars has different layers, including a metal core made from iron and nickel, a thick, rocky middle section, and a thinner crust. Although the atmosphere of Mars is nothing like Earth's. It's made from carbon dioxide, nitrogen, and argon gases and is very thin.

The planet Mars is dry, rocky, and cold.

Because of its thinness and **composition**, Mars's atmosphere doesn't protect the planet from meteorites, comets, and other objects zipping through space the way Earth's atmosphere does. Mars's atmosphere also doesn't trap heat from the Sun very well, so the temperature on Mars can be bitterly cold. An afternoon on Mars can be a freezing −28°F (−33°C). At night, the temperature often dips to an even more frigid −225°F (−143°C)!

Earth, on the other hand, is warm and wet.

DID YOU KNOW?

If Earth were the size of a nickel, Mars would be about as big as a dime!

The RED PLANET

Mars is commonly known as the Red Planet, but its surface is many colors, including gold, tan, and brown. The red color comes from a large amount of iron in Martian rocks. The iron oxidizes, or rusts, resulting in the reddish color. Dust forms after the rocks break down. Then the dust floats into the air during storms, which are common on Mars, and fills the atmosphere. From a distance, this makes the planet look almost entirely red. Besides the rocks and dust, Mars's landscape has some incredible features. One of the most impressive is a volcano that's the largest in the solar system! Named Olympus Mons, it's three times taller than Mt. Everest on Earth. Its base alone is as big as the state of New Mexico. Mars also has two polar ice caps made of frozen carbon dioxide, or dry ice, plus some regular frozen water. Moreover, Mars has a string of deep canyons that are long enough to stretch from New York to California. The deepest of the canyons is ten times bigger than America's Grand Canyon.

Mars's huge canyon shown here is called Valles Marineris.

MOONS OF MARS

Mars has two rocky moons called Phobos and Deimos. They're shaped like potatoes and may have once been large asteroids! Phobos, the larger moon, is covered with deep craters and grooves. It's slowly getting closer to Mars, and scientists predict it will crash into the planet in about 50 million years. Deimos is approximately half the size of Phobos and is more irregularly shaped but with a smoother surface.

Phobos, one of Mars's two moons

MARS in HISTORY

Humans have been fascinated by Mars since ancient times. In fact, the Romans named Mars after their god of war because the planet's red color made them think of blood. Before the Romans, the Ancient Egyptians referred to Mars as *Her Desher*, which means "the red one." For hundreds of years, people have wondered if there could be life on Mars. In the late 1800s, **astronomers** guessed that Mars had once been covered with water. Giovanni Schiaparelli used **refracting** telescopes to map out the surface of Mars. He saw long grooves carved into the surface of the planet and called them *canali*, the Italian word for "channels." Some scientists mistakenly thought the channels did not form naturally. They **speculated** that intelligent beings lived on Mars and built the channels. "That Mars is inhabited by beings of some sort or other we may consider as certain," said astronomer Percival Lowell in 1906. The idea of intelligent life-forms on Mars stuck in people's minds for centuries.

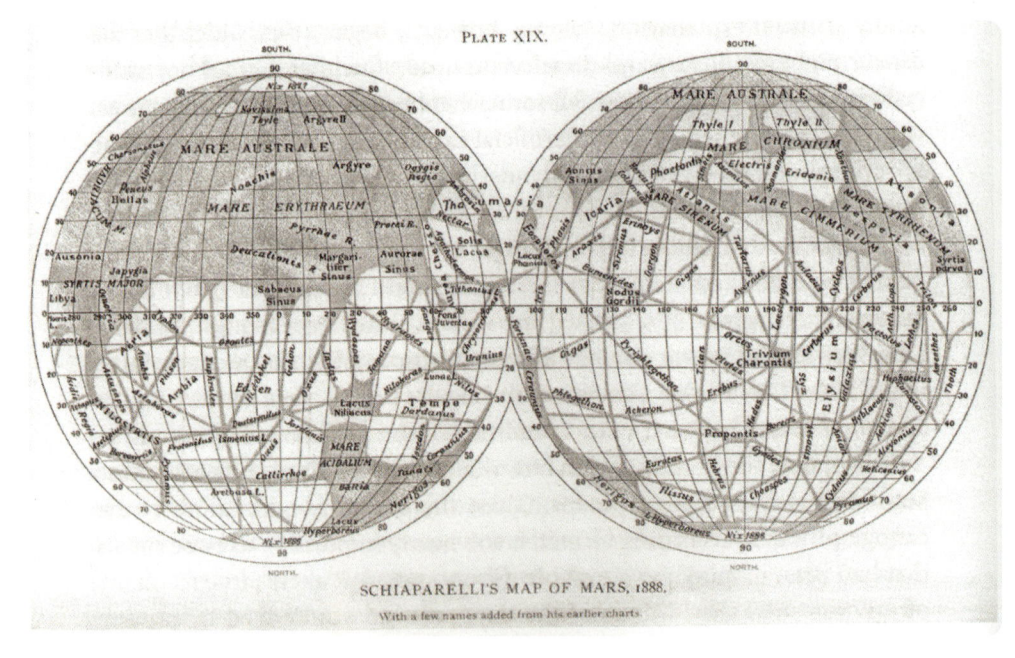

One of Giovanni Schiaparelli's maps of Mars

EARLY TELESCOPE TECHNOLOGY

The earliest telescopes used lenses to gather more light than the human eye could. They focused the light to make distant objects appear brighter, clearer, and magnified. This type of telescope is known as a refracting telescope. Most refracting telescopes use two main lenses. The larger lens is called the objective lens, while the smaller one used for viewing is called the eyepiece lens. The size of the image produced by a lens is in relation to the focal length of the lens. The focal length is the distance between the center of the lens and whatever it's focusing on. The longer the focal length, the larger the image appears!

Percival Lowell uses a refracting telescope in 1914. He wrote three popular books about Mars. One 1908 book was called *Mars as the Abode of Life*.

Since Schiaparelli and Lowell's time, people have continued to wonder about intelligent life on Mars. In books and movies, they imagined green-skinned Martians and bustling **futuristic** cities. They also investigated the idea of people **colonizing** Mars. In the 1940s, rocket scientist Werner von Braun, who later became known as the father of space travel, wrote a book about sending humans to Mars. He called it *The Mars Project*. In the book, he laid out detailed technological plans to build a spacecraft and send it to Mars. His plan involved a fleet of 10 spacecraft and 70 crew members that would spend 443 days on Mars. The supplies needed for the voyage would be prepped on Earth and sent to Mars using launch vehicles powered by special fuel. After reaching Mars, the crew would then use telescopes to find a landing site. Although there were shortcomings in his plan, Von Braun's work greatly influenced NASA's future exploration of Mars.

Werner von Braun standing next to a rocket

DID YOU KNOW?

In 1938, filmmaker and writer Orson Welles read the science fiction story "The War of the Worlds" on the radio. The radio show caused widespread panic. Some Americans listening to it thought that Martians were real and actually invading New Jersey!

A movie poster for *The War of the Worlds*

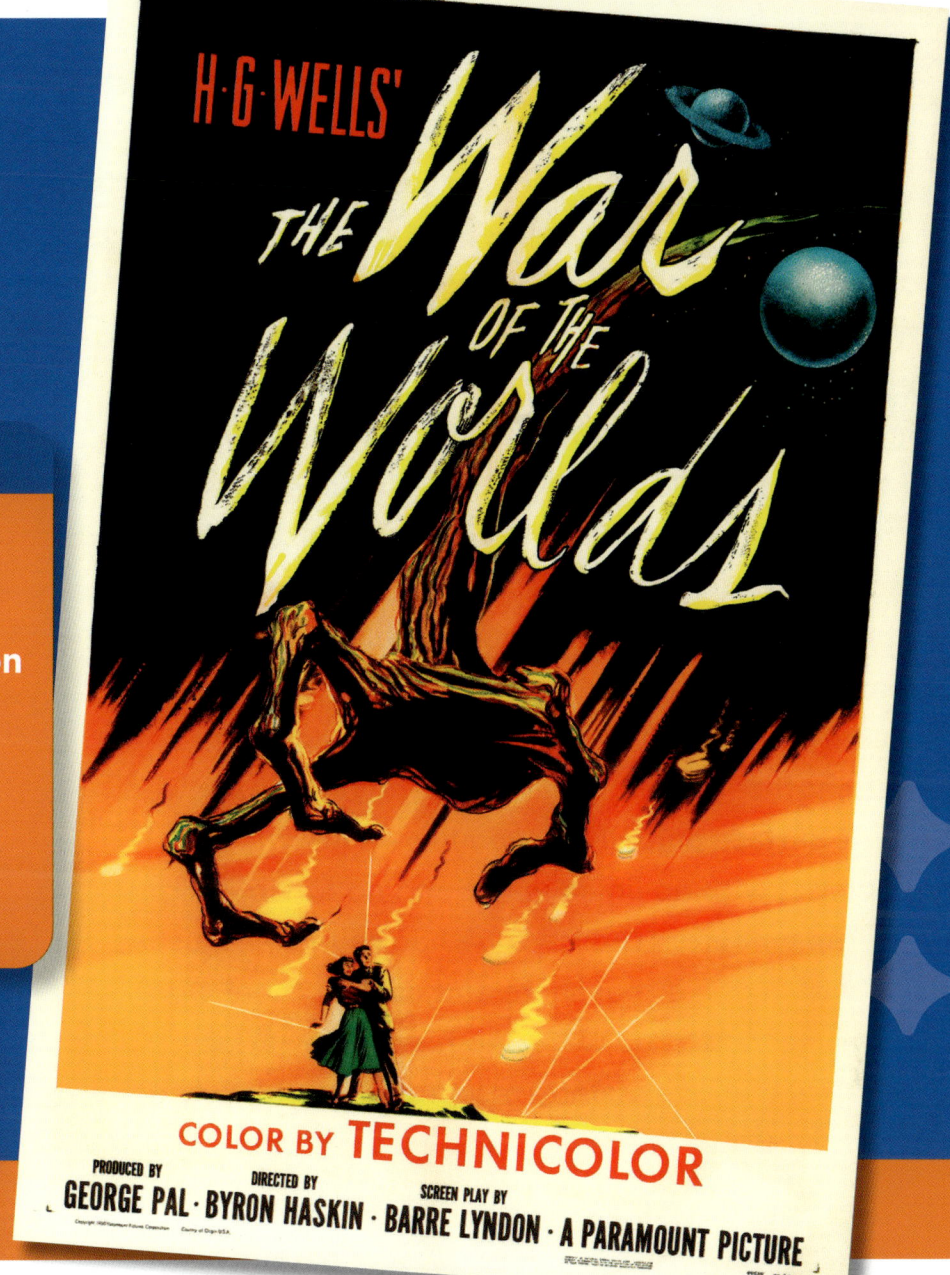

REACHING MARS

Starting in the 1960s, scientists built spacecraft in hopes of reaching Mars. Mars is about a hundred times farther away than the Moon, so it is much more difficult to send spacecraft there. There were 13 of these early missions and not all were successful.

Some of the space probes exploded, broke down, or got stuck in *orbit* around Earth. In 1964, NASA successfully launched Mariner 4. The Mariner spacecraft had a main octagon-shaped section that housed all the electronics needed to control and steer the probe. Attached to this were antennas to communicate with the team back on Earth and cameras. The probe also had four solar panels that harnessed the Sun's energy for power. Mariner 4 was carried into space on a rocket and reached Mars in 1965. It performed a flyby of the Red Planet, capturing the first images of another planet from space! The photos showed what Mars's surface actually looked like—a heavily cratered planet with no liquid water and no obvious signs of past or present life. "The Mars we had found was just a big moon with a thin atmosphere and no life. There were no Martians, no canals, no water, no plants, no surface characteristics that even faintly resembled Earth's," said NASA scientist Bruce Murray.

The launch of Mariner 4

DID YOU KNOW?

Mounted on Mariner 4 was a cosmic dust collector. Its job was to measure the speed, distribution, density, and direction of dust in space.

Scientists assembling Mariner 4

Mariner 9

Despite not finding any signs of life, the Mariner 4 mission was still considered a great achievement. Many technological advancements were made, and scientists learned how to deliver future missions to Mars. For the first time, NASA scientists were able to change the path of the spacecraft while it was in deep space. Also, Mariner 4 was only planned to work for eight months in orbit but lasted for three years! During that time, it gathered a wealth of information about Mars's atmosphere, the planet's mass, and solar winds.

After Mariner 4, NASA built other interplanetary probes. In 1971, the more advanced Mariner 9 probe traveled through space to study Mars. It photographed Mars's surface and analyzed the planet's atmosphere. Its work was interrupted by a huge dust storm covering the entire planet. After the dust settled, Mariner 9 took images that revealed a Martian landscape covered with dry lakes and riverbeds—evidence that Mars once had water, lots and lots of it.

SOLAR WIND

Solar wind is a speeding stream of particles and radiation released by storms on the Sun. It can whip at almost a million miles per hour! The particles can bombard everything in the solar system, including the planets. Earth's atmosphere has a magnetic field that blocks solar wind. The magnetism comes from Earth's metal core. However, sometimes solar wind can disrupt telecommunications satellites, causing cell phone issues. It can also interfere with power grids on Earth and cause blackouts. Mars has no such magnetic field. When solar winds reach Mars, they can destroy what's left of the planet's atmosphere.

What a solar wind storm might look like

CHAPTER 3
LIFE on MARS?

Future missions to Mars further investigated the possibility of life there. One of the most exciting was NASA's Project Viking. It took place between 1975 and 1982. Twin spacecraft, Viking 1 and 2, traveled to Mars to study and photograph the planet's surface. Viking 2 landed while the other probe orbited the planet. Both spacecraft were powered by plutonium, a radioactive metal that gives off heat as it breaks down. It's the same fuel used to power some nuclear reactors on Earth. This power source allowed Viking 1 and 2 to carry out long-term studies. The probes monitored the weather to see if it could be **hospitable** to life. Viking 2 tested the Martian soil and discovered unusual chemicals. It was not clear if these chemicals had come from living things. This led scientists to conduct many tests. Their findings didn't lead to any firm conclusions. However, it left them wondering if radiation from the Sun entering Mars's thin atmosphere had destroyed any evidence of tiny living things that had once been in the ground.

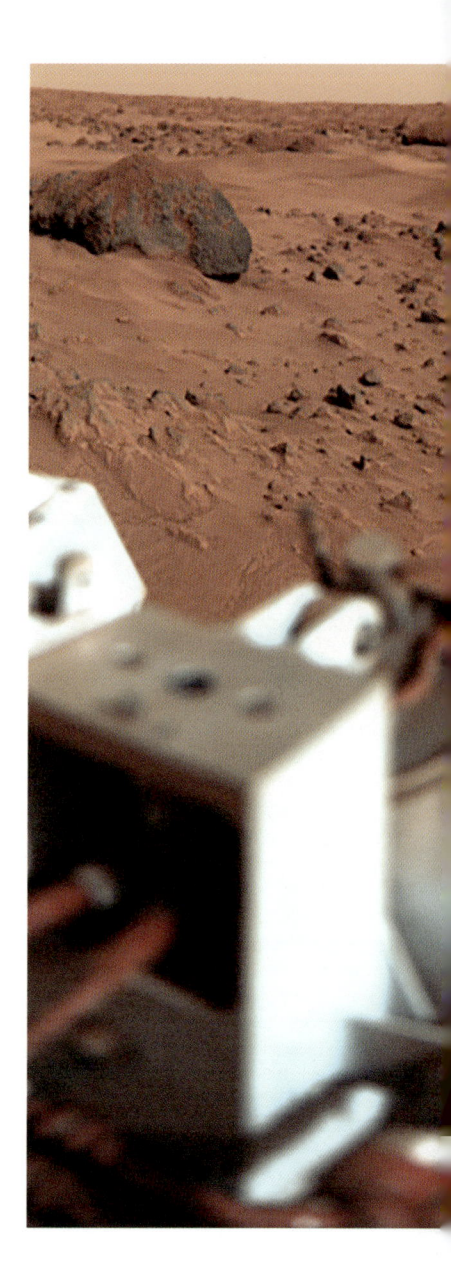

DID YOU KNOW?

In 1976, the Viking mission captured an image of what looks like a human face on Mars. People went wild. Some thought it was evidence of life on Mars. In reality, the so-called face was created by light and shadows on rocks.

An image taken by Viking 2

23

METEORITE from MARS

After the Viking probes, there wasn't a successful mission to the Red Planet for another two decades. NASA launched the Mars Observer in 1992, but it was lost in space. NASA reexamined its plans to explore Mars. In 1996, scientists made a thrilling discovery—on Earth. They had found a meteorite in Antarctica that had originally come from Mars! The grapefruit-sized rock formed on Mars 4.5 billion years ago. They could tell that the rock came from Mars—and how old it was—by the mix of dust particles it contained. Scientists think Mars was once warm like Earth with a thick protective atmosphere. The sky was blue and similar to our own. Rivers, lakes, and oceans likely covered the Red Planet's surface. At some point, Mars's climate drastically changed. The planet went from a warm, wet place to a barren, dusty, and freezing world. Scientists are still unsure why this happened. However, the meteorite helped provide some clues.

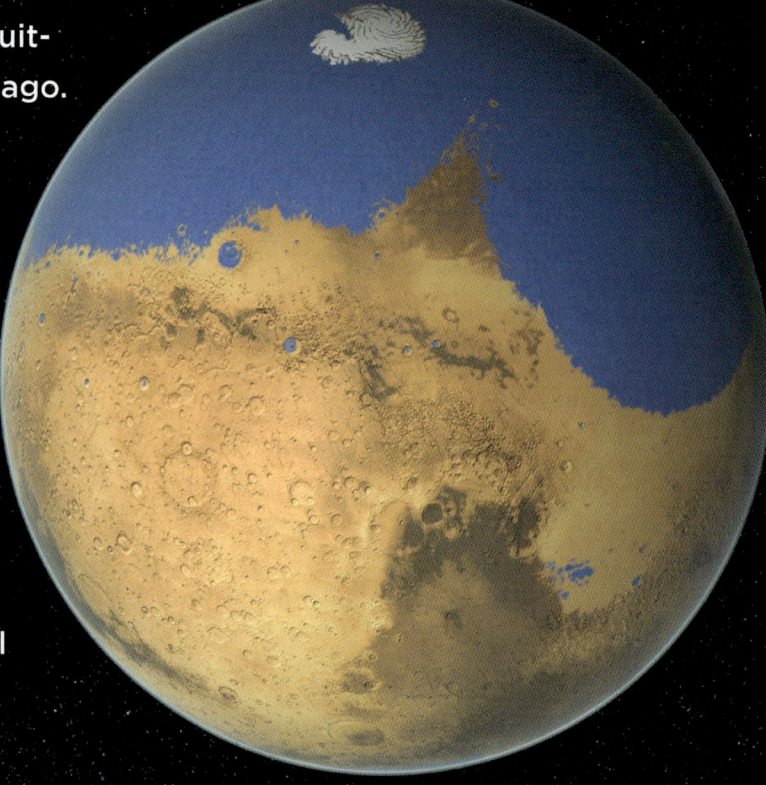

This image shows what Mars might have looked like when it was covered with water.

EXPLORER CARL SAGAN

Astronomer Carl Sagan (1934–1996) was a leading scientist who advanced our understanding of life in the universe and space exploration. He was especially interested in searching for life on other planets. Sagan said, "The nature of life on Earth and the search for life elsewhere are two sides of the same question—the search for who we are." He believed humans would find evidence of life on Mars. He helped design and manage two missions to Mars, Viking 1 and 2. He also linked the seasonal changes on Mars to windblown dust.

Here is Carl Sagan (center) with other scientists.

Scientists believe that around 15 million years ago an asteroid or comet slammed into Mars. The impact was so great it caused the Martian rock to fly into space. It eventually found its way to Earth, where the meteorite crashed into Antarctica about 11,000 years ago. Scientists wonder if an impact from an asteroid or comet could have blown away part of the Martian atmosphere, leading to a dramatic shift in the climate.

This is an enlarged piece of a fragment from the Martian meteorite known as ALH84001.

DID YOU KNOW?

While Mars currently does not have a magnetic field, some parts of the planet are magnetized. This could indicate that the planet's magnetic field was intact four billion years ago.

The chain-like structures found in the Martian meteorite resemble living organisms.

That wasn't the only surprising discovery. When scientists took a closer look at the Martian meteorite, they found it contained some unusual tiny structures. The structures resemble bacteria found on Earth as well as **by-products** of those bacteria. Research teams used a sophisticated microscope to closely examine the meteorite and its super small structures. While they were unable to conclude whether life existed on Mars, they were energized to continue their search.

MARS
PATHFINDER

About a year after the discovery of the Martian meteorite, the Mars Pathfinder and its much smaller 23-pound (10-kg) rover, Sojourner, "bounced" down on Mars. The Pathfinder was fitted with airbags that cushioned its landing. Because of its size, Sojourner was easily able to navigate Mars's rocky surface. It used a machine called an x-ray spectrometer to make out the composition of soil and rocks. It also took photos of a valley that clearly showed water had carried rocks there. People followed Sojourner's travels on the internet. Together, the two probes collected more than 10,000 images of Mars. Other missions followed, revealing the possibility of life in the Red Planet's polar ice caps and in vents near Mars's core.

Both the Pathfinder and Sojourner (pictured here) rovers had solar panels for power.

IS THERE WATER ON MARS TODAY?

The answer is yes! There is water on Mars, but *liquid* water doesn't exist for very long because of the thin Martian atmosphere. Any pure water evaporates so quickly that it jumps from ice to gas, skipping the liquid phase. Some frozen water can be found under the surface of the polar ice caps. It's also found as salty water that sometimes flows down hillsides and craters, leaving visible streaks. "Now we know there is liquid water on the surface of this cold, desert planet," said NASA scientist Michael Meyer. "It seems that the more we study Mars, the more we learn how life could be supported and where there are resources to support life in the future."

Mars's northern ice cap

MARS EXPLORATION ROVERS

In the early 2000s, NASA introduced the Mars Exploration Rovers, or MERs, named Spirit and Opportunity. These identical rovers had even more tools than past rovers, including an amazing robotic arm. Similar to a human arm, the robotic arm had three joints: a shoulder, elbow, and wrist. The arm could twist, bend, and extend to gather rock samples. That's not all. The robotic arm was equipped with a small grinding instrument called the Rat Abrasion Tool (RAT). It carefully collected rocks as a geologist would on Earth. The MERs also had two spectrometers to analyze the makeup of rocks plus a microscopic imager to provide extremely close-up images of the rocks and soil.

This is an illustration of a MERS rover on Mars.

The rovers' powerful computer "brains" allowed them to communicate with crews back on Earth and monitor their own "health" status, making adjustments as needed. Among many other functions, they stored information away from the Sun's damaging radiation. Thanks to Spirit and Opportunity's work, scientists were able to gather even more data about Mars and concluded that some Martian rocks had been soaked in water. "It changed their texture, and it changed their chemistry. We've been able to read the telltale clues the water left behind," said a MERs team leader.

Opportunity worked longer than any other rover on Mars—more than 14 years! These are its tracks on the planet. Spirit lasted six years.

DID YOU KNOW?

The robotic arm has a small brush connected to the grinding tool or RAT. The brush sweeps away any leftover rock on the tool for peak performance. In a way, the RAT has its own toothbrush!

CURIOSITY

To show the different sizes of the rovers, two Jet Propulsion Laboratory engineers stand with Curiosity on the right and Spirit and tiny Sojourner on the left.

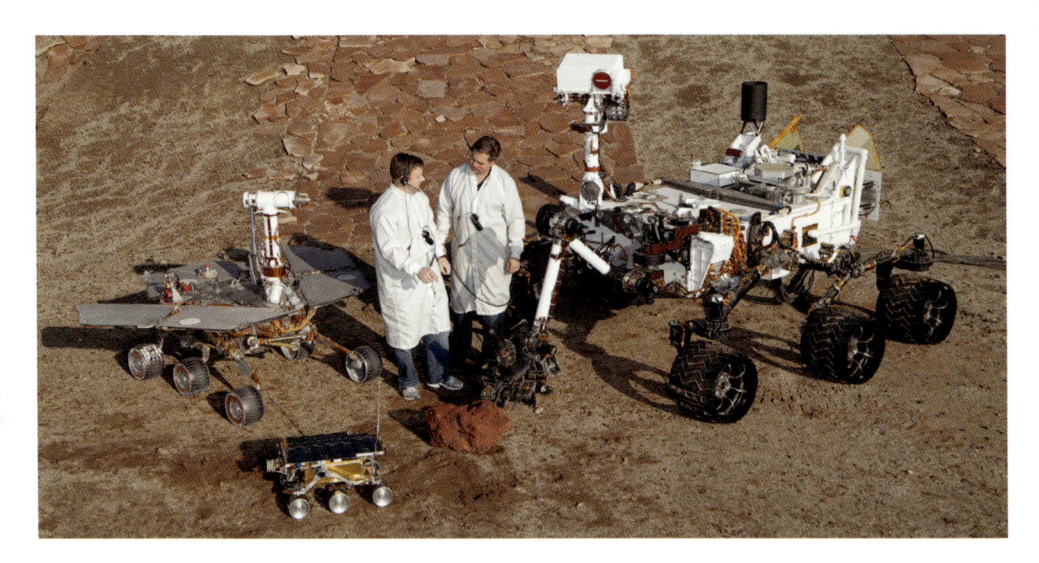

In 2012, Curiosity, NASA's largest rover to date, landed on Mars. The rover is as big as a car and as tall as a basketball player! Thousands of people gathered in New York City's Times Square to watch the touchdown on a giant screen. After Curiosity safely landed, they eagerly chanted, "SCI-ence, SCI-ence, SCI-ence!"

Carrying loads of equipment, including 10 different scientific tools and a 7-foot (2-m) robotic arm, Curiosity got to work analyzing the Martian environment. One of Curiosity's most fascinating discoveries was measuring radiation levels and finding they were similar to those on the International Space Station (ISS). Because astronauts can safely tolerate the radiation levels on the ISS, humans might be able to explore Mars one day. Curiosity also explored a streambed, where water had once flowed for thousands of years. Moreover, it kept track of the weather on a daily basis and recorded seasonal changes. As of 2022, the Curiosity rover is still investigating Mars and moving much faster and farther than earlier rovers.

RADIATION AND ITS RISKS

Curiosity used one main tool for studying the radiation levels on Mars. It's known as RAD, or the Radiation Assessment Detector, and is about as big as a small toaster. This instrument measures the types and amount of harmful radiation on Mars. These radiation types include tiny particles called protons and neutrons as well as gamma rays. Gamma rays are an extremely powerful type of light. The radiation comes from the Sun and other things in space, such as exploding stars called supernovas. Space radiation can be very dangerous to humans. It can cause some serious health problems, such as cancer and heart disease, and can be deadly in high enough doses.

The Curiosity rover takes a selfie!

In 2021, the Perseverance rover joined Curiosity on Mars. For about two years, Percy the rover explored the surface of Mars, starting in the Jezero Crater. Using its robotic arm, it will drill into ancient Martian rock to gather **core samples**. It will also collect dust from Martian rocks and soil to look for signs of ancient life. Perseverance has the technology to then store the core samples in sealed tubes until they can be collected by scientists and analyzed back on Earth. The rock samples will help scientists recreate what Mars's environment was like a long time ago.

This is a close-up of Perseverance's powerful drill.

Ingenuity, the Mars helicopter

Perseverance is also carrying new technology that may pave the way for humans to visit Mars. Attached to the rover's underside was a small helicopter called Ingenuity. On April 19, 2021, Ingenuity took flight and made history. It was the first-ever powered flight in Mars's thin atmosphere! The test flight will be helpful for future missions. The helicopter provides scientists with a bird's-eye view of Mars. Helicopters might also be utilized in the future to carry supplies around the planet. "We don't know exactly when Ingenuity will lead us, but today's results indicate the sky—at least on Mars—may not be the limit," said Steve Jurczyk, a NASA official.

DID YOU KNOW?

Mars completes its orbit around the Sun every 687 days. So a year on Mars lasts 687 Earth days. However, Mars spins at the same rate as Earth, so a Martian day lasts about as long as an Earth day!

CHAPTER 4
FUTURE EXPLORATION

Each mission to Mars—from Mariner 4 all the way up to Perseverance—is the result of hard work and information gathered from past missions. Every flyby and rover trip has allowed scientists to gain more knowledge about the mysterious Red Planet and increased their hopes of one day traveling there. However, getting to Mars presents multiple challenges. Even though Mars is the most hospitable planet in the solar system next to Earth, it's still a very harsh place that's tens of millions of miles away. The trip would take anywhere from five to ten months. Scientists would need to build a spacecraft that can safely transport people and carry enough fuel to reach the planet. They'd also need to figure out how to protect the spacecraft and people inside from extreme heat when speeding through Mars's atmosphere.

Another big concern is the health and safety of astronauts once they get to Mars. Spending several months—or even years—in deep space can greatly impact a person's physical and mental health. For starters, being confined to a small spacecraft with other people can cause stress and anxiety. There's also the issue of living in an environment with less gravity. On Mars, everything weighs about one-quarter of what it does on Earth. This low gravity can result in loss of bone and muscle mass and heart and eye problems.

For as long as humans have been dreaming about Mars, they've wanted to visit the planet. This is an artist's impression of what a human habitat on Mars might look like.

A SpaceX launch

Perhaps the greatest risk to human health is radiation from the Sun and other objects in space. Astronauts would be exposed to radiation during the trip to Mars and could develop radiation-related health issues even before they set foot on the planet. Then they would be further exposed during any extended stay on Mars. Also, the atmosphere of Mars has no breathable oxygen, and there's no drinkable water on the surface of the planet.

Scientists agree one of the keys to survival on Mars is technology. There are many proposed technological solutions to the problems mentioned, but all require a great deal of money. It's thought that sending humans to Mars could cost a minimum of $250 billion. Many nations and space agencies, including NASA, along with several private companies are working to make this pricey dream a reality. One such company is called SpaceX. Another is called Blue Origin.

GOT OXYGEN?

Because the Martian atmosphere is mostly carbon dioxide (CO_2), scientists need to come up with a way to make oxygen for breathing. One of their solutions is a machine called the Mars Oxygen In-Situ Resource Utilization Experiment, or MOXIE for short. MOXIE takes CO_2 from Mars's air and then splits the molecules into oxygen and carbon monoxide. The oxygen is captured and the carbon monoxide and other exhaust are released. MOXIE could be used on a large scale to provide oxygen for astronauts to breathe on Mars. Moxie could also make enough oxygen to burn as rocket fuel for the astronauts' return trip to Earth.

Scientists work on MOXIE at the Jet Propulsion Laboratory.

GETTING to MARS

SpaceX has designed a spacecraft called Starship. It's the most powerful and tallest rocket ever built. Starship can carry people and supplies on long voyages to the Moon, Mars, and beyond. Starship will have an extra-protective heat shield so that it can enter and exit Mars's atmosphere many times without being damaged. It will also have the capacity to use the gases from Mars's atmosphere to make its own fuel.

SpaceX Starship

NASA is also leading a new program called Artemis to make human spaceflight to Mars possible. The first stop is not Mars, however. It's the Moon! They would reach the Moon using a new vehicle called the Orion Spacecraft and then gradually build a lunar space station called Gateway. From there, NASA plans to use a special transportation vehicle to ferry astronauts from Gateway to the Moon. Once on the Moon, the astronauts would build a base camp where they can live, work, and learn all they can about living in space. Their objective is to use that information to prepare and send the first astronauts to Mars.

This is a representation from NASA of what a dwelling on Mars could look like.

DID YOU KNOW?

NASA has also been simulating what it would be like to live on Mars back on Earth! In 2021, they built the Mars Dune Alpha module and invited volunteers to live inside it for one year. The habitat recreates what life on Mars might be like.

41

MARS and BEYOND

The goal of SpaceX and some other private companies is to put people on Mars by the 2030s. "Mars is something we can do in our lifetimes," said businessman Elon Musk. Musk also has visions of creating a colony on Mars and fleets of hundreds of spacecraft. NASA scientists are less sure. There needs to be a lot more research and testing before humans can set their sights on the Red Planet. Studying the conditions on other planets can tell us a lot about what may go wrong on Earth. As Earth becomes less hospitable due to **climate change** and other factors, some people think that Mars could be a second home for humans. They are considering terraforming, which is making Mars like Earth. This would involve changing Mars's atmosphere by using special technology to possibly melt the polar ice caps and warm the planet. Then liquid water would return to Mars and maybe life, such as algae, after that. This may sound like science fiction, but look at how much science and technology have already accomplished!

A drawing of the James Webb Telescope in space

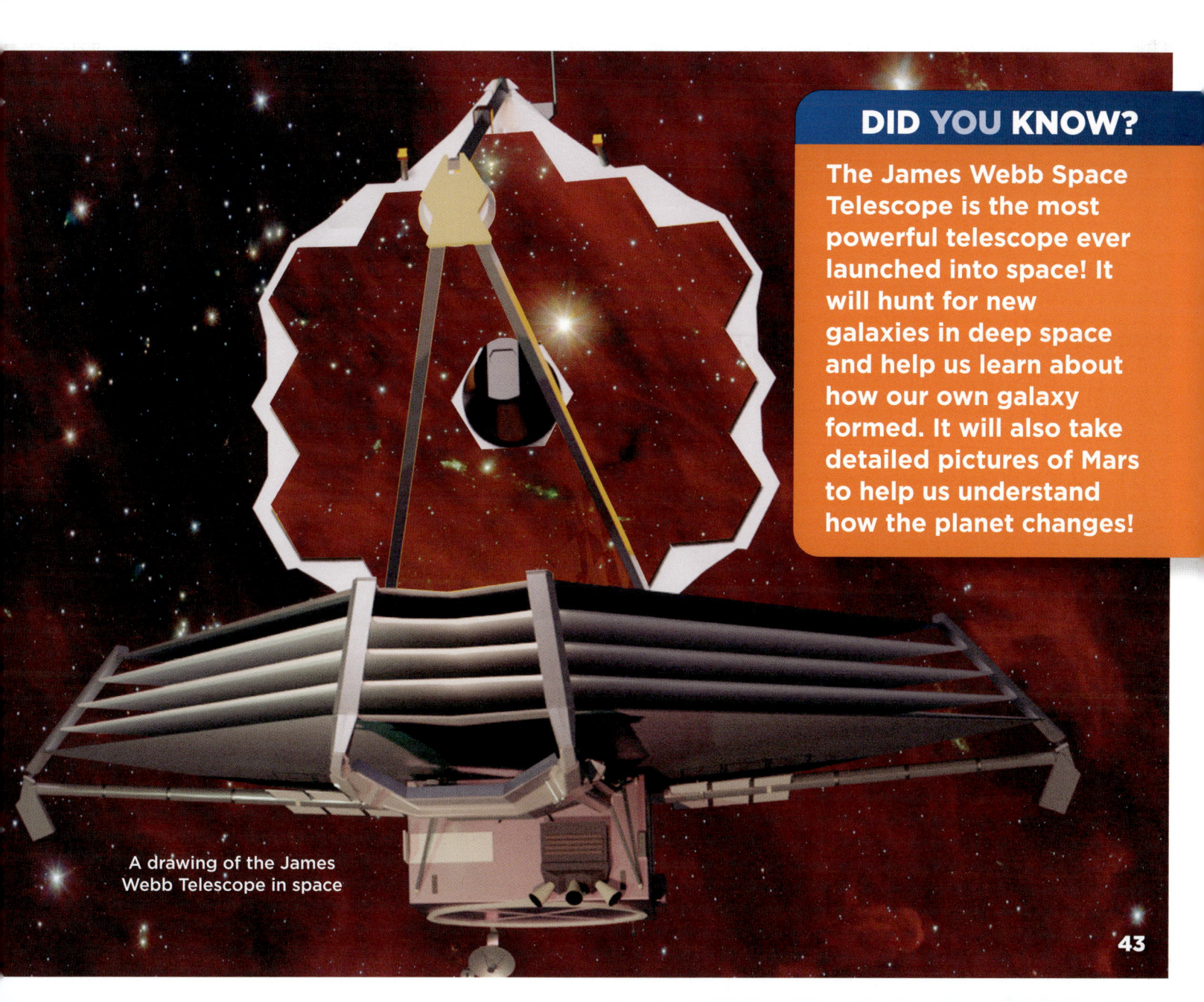

DID YOU KNOW?

The James Webb Space Telescope is the most powerful telescope ever launched into space! It will hunt for new galaxies in deep space and help us learn about how our own galaxy formed. It will also take detailed pictures of Mars to help us understand how the planet changes!

43

GLOSSARY

asteroids (AS-tuh-roidz): large and small rocky space objects that revolve around the Sun.

astronauts (ASS-truh-nawts): people who travel into space.

astronomers (uh-STRON-uh-murz): scientists who study outer space.

atmosphere (AT-muhss-fihr): the mixture of gases surrounding Earth.

bombard (bom-BAHRD): to hit something.

by-products (BAHY-prod-uhkts): things that are made as a result of something else.

climate change (KLYE-mit CHAYNJ): the warming of Earth's air and oceans due to environmental changes, such as a buildup of greenhouse gases that trap the Sun's heat in Earth's atmosphere.

colonizing (KOL-uh-nahyz-ing): settling or establishing control over.

composition (kom-puh-ZISH-uhn): the way in which a whole or mixture is made up.

core samples (KOHR SAM-puhlz): tube-shaped sections of naturally occurring substances such as rocks or ice.

deployed (di-PLOYD): sent to an area for a specific purpose.

evaporates (i-VAP-uh-rayts): turns from a liquid into a gas.

futuristic (fyoo-chuh-RIS-tik): relating to events that haven't yet happened.

geologist (jee-OL-uh-jist): a scientist who studies Earth's rocks and soil.

hospitable (HOS-pi-tuh-buhl): pleasant and favorable for living in.

lunar (LOO-ner): relating to the Moon.

microbes (MYE-krohbz): extremely tiny living things that can only be seen with a microscope.

molecules (MOL-uh-kyoolz): tiny parts made from atoms that make up everything.

NASA (NAS-ah): the National Aeronautics and Space Administration; the government agency in charge of the U.S. space program.

orbit (OR-bit): the path of an object that is circling a planet or the Sun.

probe (PROHB): a spacecraft that studies space and sends information back to Earth.

radar (RAY-dar): a tool that can find the location of an object by sending out radio waves, which hit the object and bounce back to form an image on a computer screen.

radiation (ray-dee-AY-shuhn): a kind of powerful energy made from high-energy particles.

refracting (ri-FRAKT-ing): a kind of telescope that uses a lens to change the direction of light that enters it.

satellite (SAT-uh-lite): a spacecraft sent into outer space to gather and send back information.

science fiction (SYE-uhnss FIK-shuhn): made-up stories that explore the effect that future science and technology have on people; often discusses space travel and life on other planets.

sediment (SED-uh-muhnt): tiny pieces of rock that have broken away from a larger rock; pebbles and sand are both types of sediment.

simulating (SIM-yuh-leyt-ing): imitating or pretending.

speculated (SPEK-yuh-leyt-uhd): formed without firm evidence.

terrain (tuh-RAYN): type of ground or land surface.

FOR MORE INFORMATION

Books
Aguilar, David A. *Space Encyclopedia*. Washington, DC: National Geographic, 2020.
Tour the solar system and beyond in this comprehensive book on space exploration.

Anderson, Amy, and Brian Anderson. *Space Dictionary for Kids*. New York, NY: Routledge, 2016.
Learn all about rockets, astronauts, the universe, and the fascinating world of space exploration.

DeGrasse Tyson, Neil. *Astrophysics for Young People in a Hurry*. New York, NY: Norton Young Readers, 2019.
Read about the mysteries of the universe in this accessible and exciting book.

Koontz, Robin. *Our Place in Space*. Vero Beach, FL: Rourke Educational Media, 2016.
Explore Earth's place in the universe and learn space-related facts.

Websites
NASA Kids' Club (https://www.nasa.gov/kidsclub/index.html)
NASA provides an online place for children to play as they learn about NASA and its missions.

NASA Science Space Place (https://spaceplace.nasa.gov)
NASA's award-winning Space Place website engages children in space and Earth science through interactive games, hands-on activities, and more.

National Geographic Kids—Facts About Mars (https://www.natgeokids.com/uk/discover/science/space/facts-about-mars/)
Young readers will uncover cool facts about the Red Planet.

National Geographic Kids—History of Space Travel (https://kids.nationalgeographic.com/space/article/history-of-space-travel)
Learn about the history of humans traveling into space.

Space Center Houston (https://spacecenter.org/exhibits-and-experiences/journey-to-space/)
Space Center Houston is a leading science and space exploration learning center.

Places to Visit
Kennedy Space Center in Merritt Island, FL
(https://www.kennedyspacecenter.com/?utm_source=google&utm_medium=yext)
NASA's Kennedy Space Center features exhibits and historic spacecraft and memorabilia.

The National Air and Space Museum in Washington, DC
(https://www.si.edu/museums/air-and-space-museum)
The National Air and Space Museum maintains the world's largest and most significant collection of aviation and space artifacts.

Rose Center for Earth and Space in New York, NY
(https://www.amnh.org/exhibitions/permanent/rose-center)
Explore the cosmos, the history of the universe, galaxies, Earth, and more at the Rose Center at the American Museum for Natural History.

INDEX

Artemis program, 41
Blue Origin, 38
carbon dioxide, 10, 12, 39
Curiosity rover, 9, 32–34
Deep Space Network, 7
Deimos, 13
experiments, making oxygen on Mars, 7
future exploration, 36, 38, 41–42
gamma rays, 33
Gateway lunar space station, 41
Goudge, Tim, 8
gravity, 36
Ingenuity helicopter, 35
International Space Station (ISS), 32
iron, 10, 12
James Webb Space Telescope, 43
Jet Propulsion Laboratory, 5–7
Jurczyk, Steve, 35
Lowell, Percival, 14
magnetic field, 21, 27
Mariner missions, 18–20, 36
Mars
  asteroid/comet impact and, 26
  conditions, 10–12, 21, 35, 42
  history and, 14
  polar ice caps, 12, 28–29, 42
  science fiction and, 16–17
  search for life on, 7, 18, 22, 28
  water, 8, 12, 14, 18, 20, 28–29, 31–32, 38, 42
Mars Dune Alpha module, 41
Mars Exploration Rovers (MERs), 30–31
Mars meteorite, 11, 24, 26–27
Mars Observer, 24
Mars Oxygen In-Situ Resource Utilization Experiment (MOXIE), 39
Mars Project, The (von Braun), 16
Mather, Alex, 9
Meyer, Michael, 29
Murray, Bruce, 18
Musk, Elon, 42
NASA, 4, 6–9, 16, 18, 20, 22, 24, 29–30, 32, 35, 38, 41–42
Olympus Mons, 12
Opportunity rover, 9, 30–31
Orion Spacecraft, 41
oxygen, 7, 38–39
Pathfinder rover, 28
Perseverance rover ("Percy"), 4–7, 34
Phobos, 13
plutonium, 22
radar, 5, 7
radiation, 21–22, 31–33, 38
Radiation Assessment Detector (RAD), 33
Rat Abrasion Tool (RAT), 30–31
robotic arm (on MERs), 30, 31, 34
rock samples, 7, 30, 34
safety, 36
Sagan, Carl, 25
Schiaparelli, Giovanni, 14, 16
Sojourner rover, 9, 28
solar wind, 20–21
SpaceX, 38, 40, 42
spectrometers, 28, 30
Spirit rover, 9, 30–31
Starship spacecraft (SpaceX), 40
telescopes, 14–16, 43
terraforming, 42
Viking missions, 22–23, 25
von Braun, Werner, 16
War of the Worlds radio program, 17
Welles, Orson, 17

ABOUT THE AUTHOR

Joyce Markovics has written hundreds of books for kids. She lives in an old house along the Hudson River. She is fascinated by space and all the things we still don't know about the universe. She would like to extend a Jupiter-sized thank you to Dr. Joel Green for partnering with her on this book series.